A Guide to

CW00520173

STONE CIRCLES
OF THE
LAKE DISTRICT

by
David Watson

First published in 2009 by
Photoprint Scotland

ISBN 978-0-9559438-3-6

Photographs by David & Rosemary Watson
Aerial photographs by Simon Ledingham
Graphics and design by Rosemary Watson

Cover & title page photographs: Castlerigg Stone Circle, Keswick

Printed and bound by MLG, Glasgow

CONTENTS

INTRODUCTION

The purpose of this book

There are over 50 stone circles in the Lake District, and the purpose of this guide is to introduce you to what they are, where they are and what you are likely to find, in the hope that you will develop a sense of wonder about them, sufficient to visit some of the circles yourself.

Jargon and detail are deliberately kept as simple as possible, so as to open up this complicated subject to as wide a readership as possible.

What are stone circles?

Stone circles are ancient monuments, constructed in the late Neolithic (New Stone Age) and Bronze Age periods. They are special because they are very ancient, older than the pyramids. Whilst the Great Pyramid at Giza has been dated as about 4,700 years old, Castlerigg stone circle above Keswick was built about 5,200 years ago.

The stone circle at Swinside

How were they made?

The structures were initially simple single circles or ovals, made with locally-available stones, usually about 30 or 40 forming each circle, and with a diameter of 20 to 30 metres.

Stones were usually only a metre or so high once erected, though some were up to about 3 metres.

Sometimes there would be a burial cairn or mound in the centre, and many stone circles which have been excavated show evidence of burials or cremations. Some have scatterings of stone chips, especially of the mineral quartz.

Some archaeologists identify alignment of circles and of individual stones with astronomical features, especially the positions on the horizon of the rising and setting sun and moon at different times of the year, notably the summer and winter solstice (longest and shortest days).

However, some, including one of the most eminent stones students, Aubrey Burl, dismisses most of these alignments as mere coincidence.

How did they change with time?

As time passed from the New Stone Age (Neolithic) to the Bronze Age, circle building became more precise, and some were built with double or even triple rings. Although most circles remained at about 25 metres diameter, some, such as Avebury in Wiltshire, and Long Meg in Cumbria became very large, at 100 metres or more. The early circles were special to Britain, but later versions appeared in Brittany, northern Spain and Scandinavia.

Later circles were often very small, perhaps being single-family structures. By about 1500 BC, the building of stone circles seems to have stopped.

Long Meg and her daughters, the very large stone circle near Little Salkeld

What was the function of stone circles?

This is the sixty-four-thousand dollar question, and the answer is that, in truth, nobody knows, and there is much debate. So you also can visit the stones and wonder, perhaps in awe, about what went on at these places so long ago, and you too can come up with an answer.

Undoubtedly they were important enough for simple farmers to have devoted a massive amount of energy to produce. We presume they were for ritual and religious purposes, but we have no evidence. They were certainly used for burials and cremations, and frequently remains of bones, crema-tions and typical stone funerary cists (stone chests) have been unearthed within the circles.

Burial cist at Moor Divock

In spite of the modern interest in Stonehenge at the solstice, the circles had nothing whatsoever to do with modern Druids, who came on the scene 4000 years after the circles were built.

The Druids came long after the stone circles were built

There is debate amongst academics as to whether the circles have any astronomical significance. Some say "totally", whereas others say that there is no evidence whatsoever. Eminent scholar Professor Allan Thom identifies astronomical intent in their construc-tion, whereas Aubrey Burl sees mainly some sort of trading function. Recent excavations at Stonehenge perhaps point to some sort of healing function. Most stone circle enthusiasts acknowl-edge that there is at least evidence of alignment of stones with simple astronomical events such as the rising and setting of the sun and moon at important annual events such as the summer and winter solstice (longest and shortest days). Though it assumed that the circle builders had a knowl-edge of the calendar and of the seasons, the general wisdom is that the stones, their surfaces and placements are all too crude to achieve anything other than symbolic astronomy. Also, given the number of stones used, and the number of celestial bodies, it is inevitable that some alignments between stones and celestial bodies exist.

But there are others who see serious scientific purpose everywhere they look in almost all the stone circles. Anthony Weir believes that stone circles gave the priest class the ability to accurately predict eclipses, and that this knowledge gave them enormous power.

Others believe that the circles had an economic function, perhaps as meeting places. Simon Hedges from Ireland, argues that the circles merely served as cattle markets.

There is a widespread belief that Castlerigg was in some way associated with the trade in stones axes from Langdale, and that the trade was deemed so important that it needed some sort of spiritual blessing or ritualistic ceremony, and that this occurred at the stone circle. Some believe that Elva Plain circle might have had a similar significance.

There are others who are into all sorts of ley lines, unexplained forces, energy fields and the like. Though the writer is prepared to keep an open mind on the functions of stone circles, there is no scientific evidence for any of these paranormal phenomena, and belief in them remains on the fringes of stone circle study.

What the function of circles like Blakely Raise was no-one really knows

However, the truth is that we simply do not know what the circles were for, and therefore it is inevitable that people will hypothesise about all manner of possibilities. Someone out there no doubt believes that they were built by aliens as landing sites for flying saucers. And maybe they are right.

What do we invite you to do?

We suggest you visit some of these ancient sites, especially some which are a bit remote and not overwhelmed by visitors, such as Swinside or Game-lands. Spend some time there, wondering what motivated these simple Neolithic and Bronze Age farmers to create these great monuments. Maybe the reasons are ultra simple; perhaps they had knowledge and technology which is now lost. In our modern culture where we need to know the scientific reason for everything, it is refreshing, sometimes, not to know, and at least to be a little in awe of the people who came so long ago before us, and to wonder.

Cup and ring marks on Long Meg

Rock "Art", Cup and Ring Marks

Along with stone circles and standing stones there is occasionally another phenomenon, cup and ring marks.

Worked into the stones of the circles, and numerous other stones and rock exposures still in situ, one often finds patterns of shallow "cup" marks, rings and spirals. Whether these are merely art-works which have survived the several thousand years since they were patiently worked into the rock, or whether they have other purposes, there is no agreement. Literally scores of suggestions have been put forward for their use.

Cup and ring marks in Perthshire, Scotland

Some see the same astronomical purposes which they propose for stone circles, especially when the cup marks and rings are in lines. Others see nothing more than a collection of fascinating rock doodles.

On softer rocks, these marks may well have disappeared during the 4000 to 5000 years since they were made, but on harder stones they are still visible. Perhaps the most interesting site is one at Copt Howe, in the Langdale Valley, only recognised in the 1990s.

The marks at Copt Howe are on a huge boulder, probably a glacial erratic. They are quite worn, and only clearly visible in the low light conditions of early morning or just before sunset.

The Climate of the Neolithic, the so-called "Hypsithermal"

When we see the wild, wet moorland today, on which some of the stone circles such as Moor Divock and Burnmoor are located, we wonder what attracted Neolithic man, the first farmer, to such infertile and inhospitable places. The reason, of course, is that 5000 years ago, Britain was a much warmer place.

Palaeo-climatologists, looking at changes in ancient pollen remains, believe the average temperature then was perhaps 3°C above the present, making land usable for farming several hundred metres higher than now. This was the period of the so-called "hypsi-thermal", the temperature high point since the last ice age. It was indeed a period of climatic optimum, giving early cultivators the best possible chances. Maybe it even "kick-started" the development of agriculture here.

Neolithic farmers sought out suitable land, and began the clearance of the forest, especially on warm south-facing slopes, such as Burnmoor above Eskdale and at Elva Plain.

As the Neolithic period was replaced by the Bronze Age, about 3500 years ago, the climate began to change again, and the warm conditions were overtaken by a time which was colder and wetter. Cultivation was no longer possible around many of the higher sites and stone circles, and large-scale human occupation in these places was abandoned.

Climate changes dramatically with altitude

The Stones and the rocks

Different parts of Lakeland have different types of rocks. The high central area is dominated by the ancient Borrowdale Volcanics, whereas the mountains of the north are mainly slightly softer Skiddaw Slates. To the south are the softer sandstones and siltstones around Coniston and Windermere, and to the east and north are a mixture of limestones and former desert sandstones.

All these rocks are several hundred million years old, and during the last million years the whole area has been repeatedly glaciated. About 10,000 years ago, the last Ice Age ended, leaving a landscape littered with glacial debris, frequently in the form of huge boulders, called erratics.

Shap Granite showing phenocrysts

As a general rule, the stone circles of the Lake District were made from the rocks which were locally available. However, in some areas, where there was a selection of possible rock types, there were particular stones of choice. This is especially the case with the circles in the east, where the distinctive Shap granite was used, with its large pink crystals of the mineral feldspar, called "phenocrysts" standing

out from the rest. When polished these make beautiful stones.

Swinside slate

During glaciation, ice moving out from the central Lake District, picked up and smoothed rocks, which were eventually deposited some distance from their original source. In some areas even today, Shap granite boulders lie scattered over the landscape where the ice deposited them. Even in areas of available Carboniferous limestone, the distinctive and harder granite seems to have been the preferred rock.

Skiddaw slate is used for all the stones of Castlerigg near Keswick, and a similar slate is used at Swinside in the southern Lake District.

At Birkrigg Common, near Ulverston, all the stones are made of the local Carboniferous limestone.

Grey Croft at Sellafield is built of stones made of volcanic agglomerate, material fused together from a mixture of boulders and lava erupted from an active volcano. As with the Shap granite boulders, the stones were probably delivered courtesy of the Ice Age.

At Long Meg near Penrith, all the circle stones are made of the granitic rock rhyolite, which is a similar pink colour to Shap granite, but more finely grained. The outlier, Long Meg, is made of the local sandstone, and may have been positioned at a later date.

The rounded river pebbles of Mayburgh Henge

Long Meg made of local sandstone

around the base.

In some cases the distinctive white mineral quartz, though seldom found as a standing stone, is sometimes found within the circle, usually as chippings or pebbles. It presumably was regarded as having a special value. Today we recognise quartz as being one of the very hardest and most resistant minerals.

Clearly the builders of stone circles knew their rocks, and they obviously had certain preferences. Whether this was because of hardness, physical appearance, or simply availability, we will probably never know.

Mayburgh Henge near Penrith, is made totally of millions of rounded river pebbles.

Pebbles of all sorts are also normally used as packing around the base of stones in stone circles. On occasions, when the main stones have been removed, often for building or walls, the evidence of their position remains in the form of the pebbles originally

PLEASE RESPECT THE STONE CIRCLES THEY ARE PART OF OUR HERITAGE

It goes without saying that you should not damage these monuments in any way. Leave no mark of your visit and take no souvenirs. Do not climb or even sit on the stones. Leave no litter. Do not climb over walls.

The Stone Circles
of the
Lake District

For each circle featured in the following section there is:
Classified information with location,
number of stones, circle diameter, geology

How to get there

A Simple Map

LEGEND

Sketch maps are simplified to allow you to
find the stone circles easily.

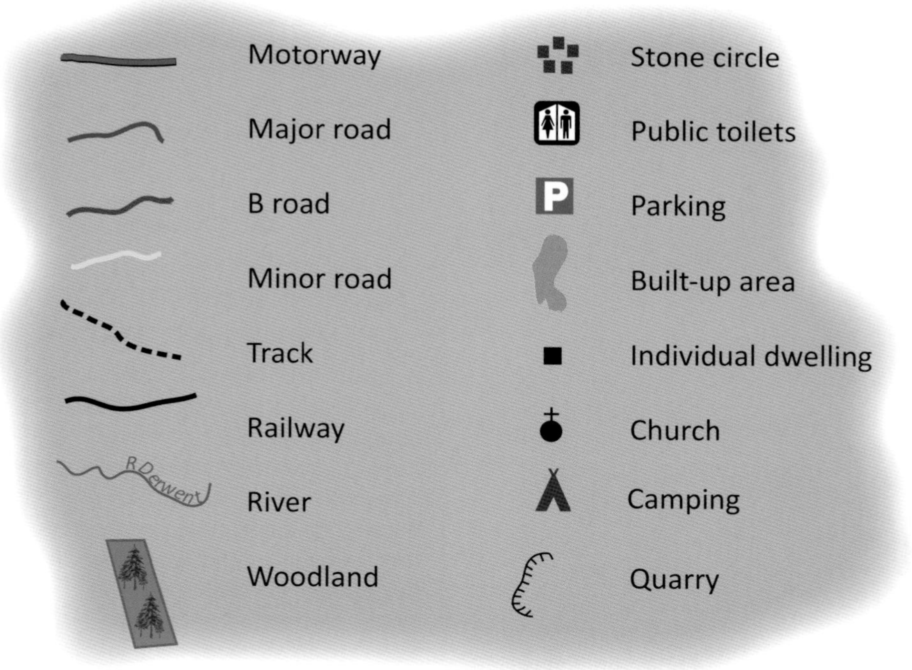
Motorway
Major road
B road
Minor road
Track
Railway
R Derwent
River
Woodland
P
Stone circle
Public toilets
Parking
Built-up area
Individual dwelling
Church
Camping
Quarry

CASTLERIGG STONE CIRCLE

CASTLERIGG also called "Keswick Carles"
Grid reference NY 291 236
Contains 38 stones, though some claim up to 40. Probably originally 41, all of local Skiddaw slate.
Diameter of circle is about 30 metres, with an unusual rectangular structure within the circle, made up of a further 10 stones.
Tallest stone is 2.3 metres. The largest stone weighs about 16 tonnes, though most are smaller. Entrance located north of the circle centre.
Age dated at about 3200BC, making Castlerigg one of the oldest stone circles in Europe.
Nearest town is Keswick

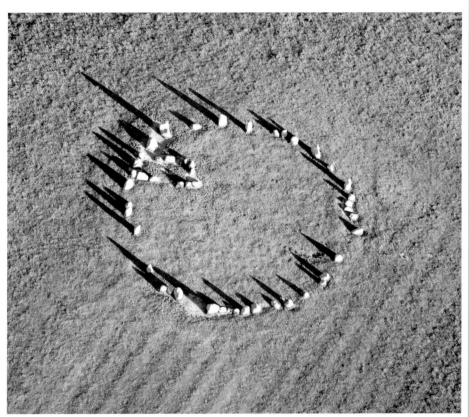

Castlerigg at sunset, aerial view looking south

Castlerigg is one of the most complete stone circles in the Lake District and is visually stunning, set on a plateau above Keswick, in an amphitheatre of hills, including Skiddaw, Blencathra and Lonsdale Fell. It is also extremely accessible, and is the most visited stone circle in Cumbria. The author has most enjoyed visiting in the early morning, when the circle has been fairly deserted. During the day it can be crowded, somewhat spoiling the peace of the place and making photography more difficult.

Apart from its size and age, Castlerigg is also distinctive in having a rectangular collection of stones within the circle on the eastern side.

The stones are made from the local slate, with the largest weighing about 16 tonnes. It is not known what the function of Castlerigg might have been, but some claim that it had a function as an observatory, with numerous astronomical alignments having been identified. Others put forward the idea that it had some spiritual function in the organisation of trade in axes or axe "blanks" from nearby Pike o' Stickle "axe factory" in Langdale valley, which supplied much of Britain. Three axes, in varying conditions, were found within the circle during 19th century excavations. Alexander Thom, one of the most eminent circle scholars, believes Castlerigg to have had importance as an astronomical observatory, and he suggests numerous significant alignments. Others, such as Aubrey Burl, believe that much of this is mere coincidence, and that at best, Castlerigg stone circle had merely symbolic astronomical significance.

Whatever its origins, Castlerigg was undoubtedly an important site for New Stone-age man. If you only visit one or two stone circles in the Lake District, make sure Castlerigg is one of them.

Castlerigg and Blencathra

THE ROMANS AND CASTLERIGG

Long believed to exist, it was not until summer 2008 that the remains of a Roman fort, presumably the "Castle.." were found just west of Castlerigg. Using modern magnetometers, Dr Mark Graham and volunteers found evidence of a camp roughly 200 metres by 200 metres close to the stone circle. However, the age of Castlerigg is underlined when we realised that even when the Romans arrived, the stone circle was already 3000 years old.

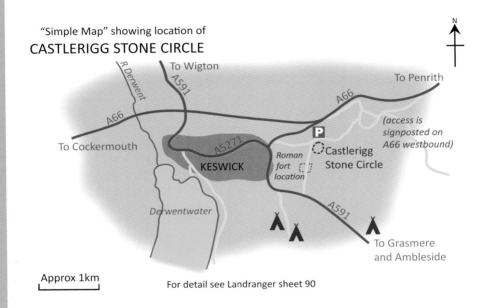

"Simple Map" showing location of
CASTLERIGG STONE CIRCLE

For detail see Landranger sheet 90

HOW TO GET THERE

a) From Keswick

Climb out of Keswick via the A591, the road for Thirlmere and Ambleside. Turn left on to the road that leads to the A66 for Penrith. After a short distance, Castlerigg is signposted to the right. The stone circle is about a mile up this road on your right. This is also one of the few circles which is well signposted.

b) You can also approach from Threlkeld and via St John's in the Vale to the east, following the signposts off the A66 from both east and west. The circle is located on a plateau at just over 200 metres, with the Lakeland fells all around. There is presently rather pot-holed parking, mainly on verges, and during the holiday season Castlerigg is usually busy. An ice-cream van keeps visitors happy during the "season". Early morning is good, but even then there are those who park up all night, especially to catch sunset and sunrise.

BURNMOOR CIRCLES

The Burnmoor Circles are located at about 250 metres above the village of Boot in Eskdale. These are the only circles featured which are accessed by a serious climb.

It seems clear that at the time these circles were built, Cumbria was experiencing its warmest climatic period since the last ice age which ended about 6,000 years or so previously, and that Burnmoor, with its gentle south-facing slopes would have been a favoured location for the early farmers. But this was short-lived, and by about 1,400 BC, the climate became colder and wetter, and the people moved to the lowlands, leaving their monuments behind.

BRAT'S HILL also known as Burnmoor. Grid reference: NY 176023 40 stones, mainly of local granite, with only 7 still standing.

Tallest stone is about 1 metre. Diameter approximately 30 metres. Nearest village Boot; nearest towns Egremont and Millom.

Burnmoor is now a wild and wet peat moorland

Brat's Hill circle is the largest of the several circles on Burnmoor, and within the circle are 5 cairns. Excavations in the early nineteenth century revealed stone cists and the usual bronze-age funerary remains, indicating cremation. There is debate about the present form of Brat's Hill, especially the rather rough and ready arrangement of the stones. Some stones students feel that the present form is a reconstruction of a previous circle, or indeed of more than one circle.

17

WHITE MOSS NE CIRCLE

WHITE MOSS known as Burnmoor D
Grid reference NY 173024
11 stones, all standing. The tallest is
just over 1 metre
Circle diameter is 16 metres
In the circle is a small cairn.

Boot village, the start of the trek

"Simple Map" showing location of
BURNMOOR CIRCLES

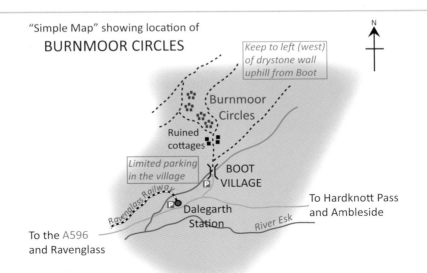

Keep to left (west) of drystone wall uphill from Boot

Burnmoor Circles

Ruined cottages

Limited parking in the village

BOOT VILLAGE

Dalegarth Station

Ravenglass Railway

To Hardknott Pass and Ambleside

River Esk

To the A596 and Ravenglass

N

Approx 1km

For detail see Landranger sheet 89

The view south from Burnmoor

WHITE MOSS SW also known as
Burnmoor C
Grid reference NY 172023
14 stones but only 2 still erect
Diameter 16 metres, as White Moss NE

LOW LONGRIGG NE together with **LOW LONGRIGG SW** are about 1km further northwest. Both are mainly in a ruinous state, and Low Longrigg SW is on a very wet site.

HOW TO GET THERE

Burnmoor is located northwest of Boot, in Eskdale, and its collection of circles involves the most arduous walk of those described in this little book. Leave the village on the track which leads directly north, going diagonally up the steep slope to Burnmoor, (shown on Landranger sheet 89 as Eskdale Moor), for just over 1km (3/4 mile). Stay west of the high wall with the fence on top. You will reach a collection of ruined huts, formerly used by peat-cutters. After a hard climb, you are almost there, with only another 500 metres of easier walking to go. The OS map here is a little simpler than the reality on the ground, but the circles are shown more or less in the right positions.

The first circle you will reach is Burnmoor, also known as Brat's Hill. Beyond it, a few hundred metres to the northwest is the White Moss pair, and about 500 metres to the north-northwest are the Low Longrigg circles.

BLAKELY RAISE

BLAKELY RAISE also called "Kinniside"
Grid reference NY 060 140
11 stones, now firmly set in concrete,
tallest about 1.15 metres. Most are of
a pink granite, with others a
fine-grained igneous rock.
Circle diameter about 18 metres.
Age: Bronze Age
Nearest village Ennerdale Bridge;
nearest town Whitehaven

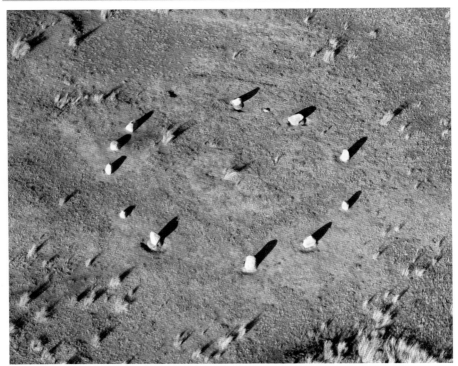

Blakely Raise - the only circle with its stones now firmly set in concrete

This is one of the few Lake District circles which have been restored, and fallen stones returned to an upright position. Blakely Raise was restored in 1925.

From its elevated location you get glimpses of the Solway and the Scottish coast beyond. One can hardly believe that the builders didn't consider the view also when they chose the location, though probably the site was wooded in Neolithic/Bronze Age times.

There are boggy areas around the circle, so although it is near to the road, don't wear your new, white trainers.

Blakeley Raise is surrounded by peat marsh

"Simple Map" showing location of
BLAKELEY RAISE STONE CIRCLE

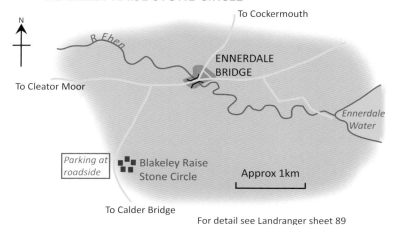

For detail see Landranger sheet 89

HOW TO GET THERE
Start at Cleator Moor, on the A5086 east of Whitehaven. Take the minor road which runs first east, and then northeast towards Ennerdale Water.

At Longmoor, just before Ennerdale Bridge, turn right for about 2 km (1.25 miles), over a cattle grid, and you will see the circle just off the road to your left.

ELVA PLAIN

ELVA PLAIN stone circle
Grid reference: NY176 317
Stones: Only 15 stones remain, out of originally about 30. All stones are now fallen, and most are low to the ground.
Diameter: a circle of about 33 metres.
Nearest village, Embleton; nearest town, Cockermouth.

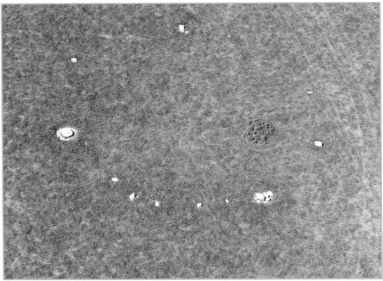

Aerial photograph showing the remains of the circle

Originally the circle would have been large and impressive. It is situated with a gently-sloping southerly aspect, allowing lovely views north to Skiddaw and also to the south of hills such as Ling Fell. In Neolithic times this might have been highly favoured farmland. The circle is big, and is of the enlarged type of the late Neolithic. Although there have been no finds of polished stone axes, "Elva" is thought to perhaps originate from the word "elfshot", a term once used for stone axes. However, this is presently just speculation. If it is true, Elva Plain may have had a similar association with the Langdale stone axes as is suggested for Castlerigg.

Though no astronomical use has been suggested for the circle, in the 1930s WD Anderson did observe a now-disappeared outlier about 55 metres to the south.

Today, visitors to the remains of the circle require a vivid imagination. Only 15 of about 30 stones remain, all of them low, recumbent or buried.

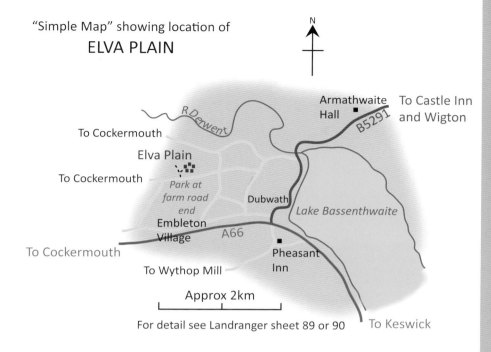

"Simple Map" showing location of
ELVA PLAIN

N

To Cockermouth

R Derwent

Armathwaite Hall · B5291

To Castle Inn and Wigton

Elva Plain

To Cockermouth

Park at farm road end

Dubwath

Lake Bassenthwaite

Embleton Village

A66

To Cockermouth

Pheasant Inn ·

To Wythop Mill

Approx 2km

For detail see Landranger sheet 89 or 90

To Keswick

HOW TO GET THERE

Leave the A66 trunk road, on to the B5291 near the Pheasant Inn, at the western end of Bassenthwaite Lake. Immediately turn left and then, after 0.5 km , turn right. After a further 1 km (just over 0.5 miles) turn left and continue for about 2 km (1.25 miles) to the entrance to Elva Plains Farm on the right. Here park your car, and follow the public footpath to the farm. Proceed along the southern edge of the farm, and through a field gate to the circle. At the entrance to the farm is a handy map, showing the path to the circle. There is no need to ask for permission.

During the author's visit the circle field was full of cows and their calves. But if you are not comfortable with cows, this might be a problem to you. The field entrance was very muddy. Wellies are sensible here in wet weather.

23

GREY CROFT

GREY CROFT also written Greycroft
Grid reference NY 033 024
10 stones out of an original 12, all
made of volcanic agglomerate except
for the most southerly, which is
sandstone.
Maximum height about 2.0 metres.
Diameter of circle about 30 metres.

The circle was restored in 1949 by
Pelham School, after an earlier farmer
had destroyed it in order to make his
ploughing easier.
From Bronze Age, confirmed by many
finds of artefacts during restoration.
Nearest village, Seascale; nearest
town, Whitehaven.

Grey Croft with Sellafield just to the north

Grey Croft has the most ironic site, one
of Britain's most ancient structures
alongside its most advanced technology at Sellafield nuclear facility.
Nothing could emphasise more just
how ancient these stone circles are,
already 2000 years old when the
Romans arrived. Like us, they probably
wondered at their construction and
possible uses.
This is also one of only a few circles
which have been recently restored,
and one wonders why not more of
Cumbria's 50 or so circles have not had
similar treatment.
Ironically, having been restored, Grey
Croft was in a sad, overgrown condi-
tion during the author's visits in 2008,
half buried in long grass and weeds.
One other thing to consider - British
Nuclear Fuels has one of the most
visited exhibitions in the Lake
District with a nice restaurant and
toilets. Why not combine 4000
year-old Grey Croft with a visit to
Sellafield and get the full flavour of the
contrast?

"Simple Map" showing location of
GREY CROFT

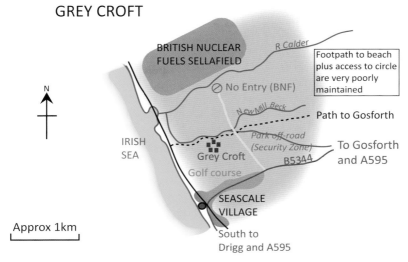

For detail see Landranger sheet 89

The Greycroft site can be quite overgrown

HOW TO GET THERE

Greycroft lies in the shadow of the southern edge of the giant Sellafield nuclear facility. If you approach from the village of Seascale, using a minor road heading towards Calder and the nuclear site, after about 1km (just over 0.5 miles) you will see a signed footpath off to the left, leading to the beach, and following the edge of Newmill Beck. The circle is off this path to the left, and there is a stile and an access path.

25

SWINSIDE

SWINSIDE also known as Sunkenkirk
Grid reference SD 172 881
55 stones, with 32 still standing.
Originally there would have been
about 60 stones.
The stones are made of the local
metamorphic slate.
Circle is about 28 metres in diameter
Tallest stone is about 2.3 metres
Age is late Neolithic-early Bronze Age,
about 3000 BC.
Nearest town is Broughton in Furness

Swinside is a complete circle in a remote and beautiful area

Visiting Swinside stone circle can be idyllic, not just because it is so complete, but also because it is peacefully isolated, in comparison with some of the more accessible, and hence more popular sites such as Castlerigg. Here there are no cars or buses, and very few visitors. In addition, some megalithic enthusiasts claim Swinside to be one of the best stone circles in Europe. Many visitors describe Swinside as being "beautiful".

Its alternative name comes from the legend that the stones were originally to be used for the building of a church (kirk). Every time they tried to build the church, the Devil caused the stones to sink into the ground, hence the name "Sunkenkirk", creating the circle which remains today. Its stones are unusually close together, a characteristic of many of the earlier circles.

Though not quite so dramatic as Castlerigg, Swinside enjoys a majestic setting, surrounded by Knott Hill and Swinside and Thwaites fells, with the Duddon estuary a few miles to the south.

Surprisingly there is little fuss made at the actual site, no signpost and no interpretation board, which many would find helpful, and which would not impinge on the atmosphere of the place.

As with a number of circles, any stones which have fallen have done so by curiously falling inwards, into the circle. The circle has an obvious entrance on the south side. Some people liken it to Ballynoe in County Down, Northern Ireland, which has many similarities. Swinside was excavated about 100 years ago. Some funerary evidence was found, in the form of charcoal and bone fragments, but nothing to suggest that the circle was a cemetery.

Fallen stones all face inwards into the circle

HOW TO GET THERE
Getting to Swinside involves a little walk of about a mile. Leave the A595 about 3 km west of Broughton in Furness at signs for Broadgate. Head up the single-track road for about 1km (just over 0.5 miles) until, just before Crag Hall, a farm track forks to the left. Here it is possible to park, if you get tight on to the verge, against the wall. (There is talk of an actual car park) Swinside Circle is along the track to the left, just under a mile and initially steeply uphill, but it is worth the walk. The circle is to the right of the track, before you reach Swinside farm.

SIGNPOSTS AND INTERPRETATION BOARDS

Visitors will be surprised, that considering Swinside Stone Circle's billing as "one of Europe's most significant neolithic monuments", there is no signpost at the site, and no interpretation board. Casual, uninformed walkers must wonder what they have arrived at.

The truth is that, at the time of writing, except for Castlerigg and King Arthur's Round Table, none of the other sites featured in this little book have any interpretative information on site. Long Meg has an erroneous sign "Long Meg Druid's Circle" (see section on Druids page 6), but unfortunately the vast majority have no information at all.

Surely we should treat these ancient monuments, which are as old or perhaps older than the Great Pyramids, in a better way.

The author would invite readers and visitors to the sites to contact English Heritage and the National Park Authority with a view to remedying the situation.

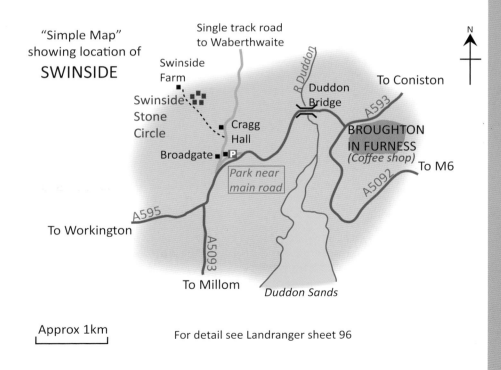

"Simple Map" showing location of SWINSIDE

Single track road to Waberthwaite

Swinside Farm
Swinside Stone Circle
Cragg Hall
Broadgate
Park near main road
To Workington
A595
A5093
To Millom

R. Duddon
Duddon Bridge
A593
To Coniston
N
BROUGHTON IN FURNESS (Coffee shop)
A5092
To M6
Duddon Sands

Approx 1km

For detail see Landranger sheet 96

BIRKRIGG

BIRKRIGG also known as "The Druids' Circle" and as "Sunbrick Circle", after the nearby farm.
Grid reference SD 292 739
Stones: 10 stones in an inner circle; 15 stones in an outer circle. All made from the local carboniferous limestone, which is relatively unusual for the Lake District.
Diameter 29 metres at its widest.
Age: Bronze Age
Nearest village Bardsea; nearest town Ulverston

Birkrigg overlooks Morecambe Bay and the village of Bardsea

Bronze Age builders must have had an eye for a view when they erected their circles. From Birkrigg you get a superb vista of Morecambe Bay, with most of your wide photos also taking in the spire of Bardsea church, together with Bardsea village.

The area was obviously of some significance to the people of the time. In addition to several tumuli (burial mounds) found around the common, excavations in 1921 revealed the use of the inner circle as a cremation site. Clearly the circle was of some importance as a ritualistic site. Coastal Bronze Age people were also great shell-fish eaters, and even 4000 years ago, Morecambe Bay would have been supplying its harvest of cockles. It is believed that shell-fish were amongst the latest additions to the human diet before the development of reliable agriculture.

"Simple Map" showing location of
BIRKRIGG COMMON

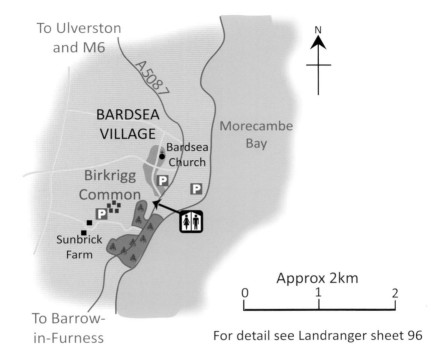

To Ulverston
and M6

A5087

BARDSEA
VILLAGE

Bardsea
Church

Morecambe
Bay

Birkrigg
Common

Sunbrick
Farm

To Barrow-
in-Furness

N

Approx 2km

0   1   2

For detail see Landranger sheet 96

HOW TO GET THERE

Head south from Ulverston on the coast road, the A5087. Only 1km (approx 0.5 miles) after the southern turn-off for Bardsea village, turn right on to an easily missed minor road, proceed uphill for 500 metres, through trees on to Birkrigg Common. This is also the access road for Sunbrick Farm. There is easy parking on the common and the circle is only about 500 metres along the minor road in a clearing to the right. It can be clearly seen, though the outer circle may be bracken-covered, depending on the time of year.

MOOR DIVOCK AND THE COCKPIT

MOOR DIVOCK is the general name for an area with 3 stone circles, numerous cairns and various Bronze age relics.
The circles are The Cockpit, Moor Divock 4 and Moor Divock 5.
All are in various states of disrepair.

THE COCKPIT
Grid reference NY 482222
About 75 stones, some standing but most lying, possibly originally in a double circle, though not obviously so now.
Diameter of circle about 28 metres.
About 300 metres above sea level.
Probably Bronze Age.
Nearest village, Pooley Bridge; nearest town, Penrith.

The Cockpit

Moor Divock has perhaps the largest concentration of Bronze Age remains in the Lake District. Within a few square kilometres there are numerous burial mounds and cairns as well as several stone circles and standing stones. Quite what made this area so special, we do not know. The circles are generally small and ruinous, but the Cockpit, which is the furthest west, is by far the most impressive.

The stones were set into a low bank, and it is believed that initially this would have been a double circle, about 31 metres diameter on the outside and 26 metres on the inside. Aerial photography best shows the circle's location.
What its purpose was is mere conjecture, but considering the large number of remains, the general area was clearly of great ritual importance.

32

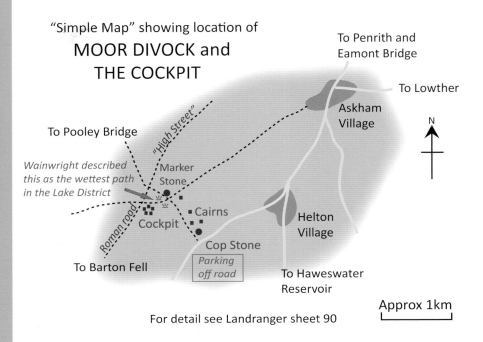

"Simple Map" showing location of
MOOR DIVOCK and THE COCKPIT

To Penrith and Eamont Bridge

To Lowther

Askham Village

N

To Pooley Bridge

"High Street"

Wainwright described this as the wettest path in the Lake District

Marker Stone

Roman road

Cairns

Cockpit

Helton Village

Cop Stone

Parking off road

To Barton Fell

To Haweswater Reservoir

Approx 1km

For detail see Landranger sheet 90

HOW TO GET THERE

The Cockpit is best accessed from the south. Take the road from Penrith to Askham and then to the village of Helton. At Helton turn right into the village and then turn right again, uphill, on the road marked "no through road". This leads to open moor, and after 1.5 km (about 1 mile) there is a public, grassy bridleway on the right, leading to Pooley Bridge. Follow the bridleway for 1.5 km until you see a small stone marker pillar in the middle of the track, just beyond a paths junction. If conditions are dry,

you can access the Cockpit via the path to the left (about 500 m). However in wet conditions, stay on the bridleway for another 500 metres before turning left onto another substantial path. The Cockpit is a further 500 metres down this path to the south, located to the left of a major paths junction.

When cloud is low or conditions are misty, it is necessary to navigate on Divock Moor using a map and compass, and because much of the area is featureless moor, it is quite easy to get lost. (Voice of experience)

34

LONG MEG AND HER DAUGHTERS

LONG MEG & HER DAUGHTERS

Grid reference: NY571 372
59 stones, of which 27 are still standing. Originally there would have been about 70 stones, the heaviest stone estimated at 29 tonnes. Long Meg is a tall stone of 3.6 metres, which stands outside the main circle. Circle diameter is between 100 and 93 metres, putting it amongst the biggest stone circles in Britain.

Long Meg is made of the local red sandstone, whereas the "daughters" are made from the granitic rock rhyolite.
There are three areas of ring markings on the northeast face of the Long Meg stone.
Believed to be Bronze Age, about 1500 to 1000 BC.
Nearest village is Little Salkeld; nearest town is Penrith.

Aerial view showing the whole circle with Long Meg herself on the outside

This is the third largest stone circle in England. Only Avebury and Stanton Drew are bigger. During most of the Neolithic period, stone circles averaged between 20 and 30 metres in diameter, but at the end of the Neolithic and during the early Bronze Age, stone circles were generally made bigger, and this is an example of one of the larger circles.

The so-called "daughters" form a slightly oval circle, longest in its east-west axis, with Long Meg, their "mother" about 25 metres outside the main circle to the southwest. This stone is of a different rock, and some suggest that it may actually be later than the circle.

The large circle is bisected by a farm road in its eastern side, but is so large that it doesn't detract from the ambience of the place.

The author's initial impression was one of some awe at the scale of the circle and the size of some of the stones, most of them many tonnes. Manoeuvring them clearly required skills which we now hand over to cranes and earth-movers.

Long Meg is sandstone, whereas the daughters are granitic rock

Long Meg and her daughters are the stuff of legend and tradition. One story goes that a coven of witches were celebrating their Sabbath, some time in the thirteenth century, and a Scottish wizard (some use the word "saint"), called Michael Scott, found them and cast a spell, turning all the witches into stone.

Another explanation is that the stones of the circle were all Long Meg's lovers. One tradition, now widespread amongst the folklore of stone circles is that the number of stones in the circle is uncountable, and anyone who tries will always get a different number. A further story says that if ever Long Meg were to be shattered, the stone will run with blood.

When you visit, you might well find "offerings" of money, quartz crystals and plants around the Long Meg stone, especially at the northeast base, left by those who believe that this is a location where one can honour and access ancient gods.

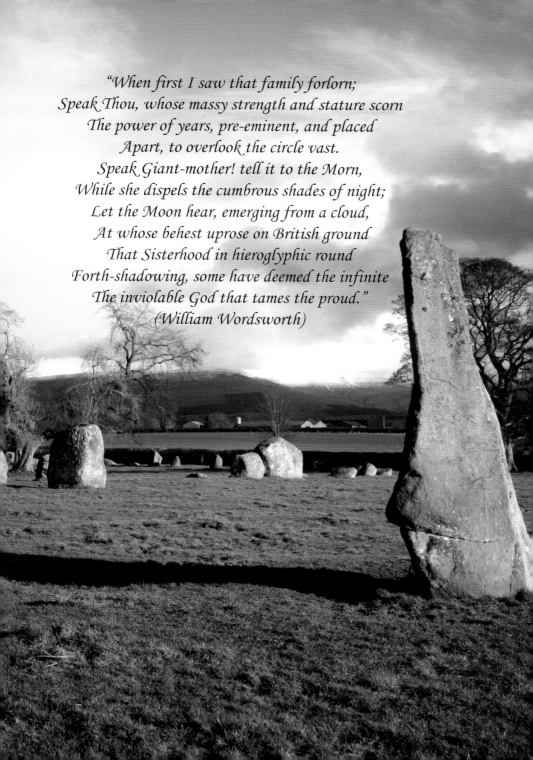

"When first I saw that family forlorn;
Speak Thou, whose massy strength and stature scorn
The power of years, pre-eminent, and placed
Apart, to overlook the circle vast.
Speak Giant-mother! tell it to the Morn,
While she dispels the cumbrous shades of night;
Let the Moon hear, emerging from a cloud,
At whose behest uprose on British ground
That Sisterhood in hieroglyphic round
Forth-shadowing, some have deemed the infinite
The inviolable God that tames the proud."
(William Wordsworth)

LITTLE MEG STONE CIRCLE is situated just 0.5 km to the northeast of the main circle. The smaller "circle" is now a jumble of stones, all having been moved from their original location to the edge of a field. On the author's visit the field entrance was a quagmire and close inspection required wearing wellingtons.

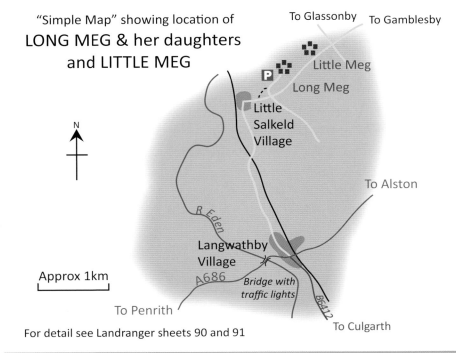

"Simple Map" showing location of
LONG MEG & her daughters
and LITTLE MEG

To Glassonby   To Gamblesby

Little Meg

Long Meg

Little Salkeld Village

N

To Alston

Approx 1km

R Eden

Langwathby Village

A686

Bridge with traffic lights

B6412

To Penrith

To Culgarth

For detail see Landranger sheets 90 and 91

HOW TO GET THERE.
Leave Penrith on the A688 to Alston. After crossing the river Eden, turn left at Langwathby to Little Salkeld. About half a mile north of the village the Stone Circle is sign-posted to the left both "Long Meg" and (erroneously) "Druid's Circle". The road crosses a cattle grid en-route to Long Meg farm. There are several small parking areas.

The signpost in Little Salkeld - but the Druids appeared thousands of years after the construction of Long Meg

GUNNERKELD STONE CIRCLE

GUNNERKELD meaning "The spring of Gunnar" (Old Norse) One of a group of "Shap " circles. Sometimes referred to as "Shap Central".
Grid reference: NY568 178
Number of stones: outer ring about 18, with only 3 still upright.
The stones have a variety of origins, and the most likely source is that they were plucked from local glacial debris as glacial erratics. (ie stones which have literally "wandered" as the ice moved out from the central fells).
A double concentric oval with outer diameter from 27 to 30 metres, and an inner diameter about 16 metres.
Age:Thought to be about 2500 BC.
Nearest village Shap; nearest town Penrith

Few travellers on the M6 even notice Gunnerkeld

Some of Cumbria's stone circles have the fascinating location of the very ancient alongside the ultra-modern, so highlighting the simplicity and antiquity of the stones. One such case is Grey Croft, next to Sellafield nuclear reactor. Another is Gunnerkeld, hard alongside the M6 motorway.
Though Gunnerkeld is mainly in ruins, it is still impressive. It is one of a small group of concentric stone circles in the Lake District, another example being Oddendale.

Looking towards Gunnerwell Farm

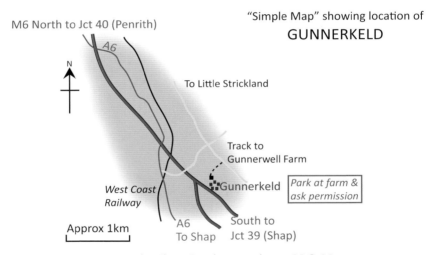

"Simple Map" showing location of
GUNNERKELD

M6 North to Jct 40 (Penrith)

A6

N

To Little Strickland

Track to
Gunnerwell Farm

*West Coast
Railway*

Gunnerkeld

Park at farm &
ask permission

Approx 1km

A6
To Shap

South to
Jct 39 (Shap)

For detail see Landranger sheets 90 & 91

HOW TO GET THERE

Drive south from Penrith on the A6 for about 10km (6 miles). 300 metres after the A6 passes *under* the M6, turn left on a minor road. Continue to a crossroads, about 1.5km (1 mile) then turn right and drive for about another 1.5km (1 mile) until you reach the sign-posted entrance to Gunnerwell Farm.

At the farm, ask permission to visit the site. The farmer, Mr Robinson, is most obliging, and access is through the woods north and west of the farm buildings, about 400 metres.

KEMP HOWE

KEMP HOWE is located just south of Shap at grid reference NY 567 133. There is not much left to see, just 6 stones in a small arc, the rest having disappeared under the railway in the 19th century, and other developments more recently.

Kemp Howe must have been very imposing before the arrival of the railway builders

Kemp Howe was once a fine stone circle, but was half destroyed by Victorian railway builders and now remains as one of several ironies, in this case the very ancient being pushed aside by the modern. Inevitably both stone circles and standing stones gradually disappear with time, especially affected by massive modern civil engineering developments such as railways and motorways. Even so, it seems rather sad that so little official attention is paid to them.

HOW TO GET THERE
Head south on the A6 from Shap village. After 1.5km (1 mile) the remaining stones of the circle are visible on the left, close to the railway line, and adjacent to the huge Corus limestone works.

41

CASTLEHOWE SCAR

CASTLEHOWE SCAR Stone Circle 10 stones all of Shap granite, and probably all glacial erratics. One outlier to north-northeast.

One stone over 1 metre still standing, the rest having fallen. Diameter varying from 6 to 7 metres. Nearest village Shap.

All that is left of Castlehowe Scar

Though totally unimpressive on its own, Castlehowe Scar stone circle is best seen as only part of the mass of megaliths which stretch from Gunner-keld in the north to Gamelands, near Orton, in the south.

The uninviting padlocked gate leading to the field containing the circle is not typical. However, the remains of the circle can be easily viewed from the common land immediately to the south.

HOW TO GET THERE

Leave the A6 at Shap village on the minor road to Crosby Ravensworth. About 1.5km (1 mile) after crossing the second motorway bridge, Castlehowe

Scar is on the right, at the junction of the road heading right (south) to Oddendale. Park just around the corner.

IRON HILL CIRCLES

IRON HILL NORTH, also referred to as *Haberwain*.
Grid Reference NY596 148
19 low stones of mixed origins (granite, limestone)
Circle diameter varies from about 11 to 14 metres.

IRON HILL SOUTH
Grid reference Ny 596 147
9 stones, mostly Shap granite, around a former cairn.
Diameter 6 to 7 metres.
The remains of a stone cist lie in the centre of the cairn

Sadly the view from Iron Hill is blighted by the enormous Corus limestone quarry

The walk uphill to the Iron Hill sites is worth the effort for the views to the east, but is spoiled by the huge Corus limestone quarry at the bottom of the hill to the west.

The circles have been much disturbed over time. Indeed, *Megalithic Portal* suggests they should be more appropriately labelled "possible robbed cairns" rather than stone circles. The more northerly site also suffers from the indignity of being dissected by a dry-stone wall.

HOW TO GET THERE

From Castlehowe Scar continue on the road towards Oddendale. At the end of the wood the road turns left. After 200 metres park at the next corner. A public footpath heads up the hill for about 300 metres to the ruined circles.

ODDENDALE STONE CIRCLE

ODDENDALE STONE CIRCLE also occasionally referred to as "Odindale" and "Odendale".
Grid reference NY 592 129
Stones: 34 in an outer circle, with smaller stones in an inner circle.
Diameter about 30 metres. Inner circle forming a kerb around a low mound 7-8 metres in diameter.
Beyond the circle to the north is another, small circle of 11 stones, mostly now buried. This arrangement is relatively unusual amongst Lake District circles.
Nearest village is Shap; nearest town is Penrith.

Sadly, all the Oddindale stones have fallen

Today the site of Oddendale occupies a sometimes windy plateau of mainly infertile land, covered in coarse grass. Only around the limestone pavements does the grass appear to get "sweeter", and is closely cropped by the sheep. But 4000 years ago, the climate was warmer here, and one can imagine a much richer and friendlier land for the Neolithic and Bronze Age farmers. Apart from stone circles there is plenty of evidence of other bronze-age activity in the area.

Along with Gunnerkeld it is an example of a double concentric ring, probably with a cairn in the centre. Evidence of cremation has been found at the site. With all the stones fallen, the present state of the circle is a bit underwhelming, but with not much imagination, one can visualise its earlier prominence in this open landscape.

"Simple Map" showing location of
CASTLEHOWE SCAR, IRON HILLS, ODDENDALE and KEMPHOWE

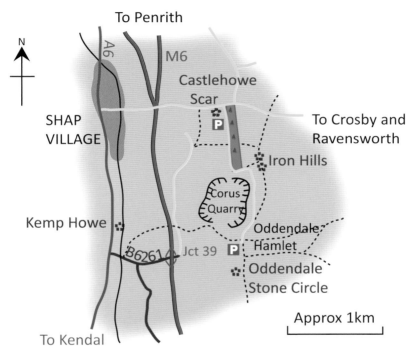

To Penrith

N

A6

M6

Castlehowe Scar

SHAP VILLAGE

P

To Crosby and Ravensworth

Iron Hills

Corus Quarry

Kemp Howe

B6261

Jct 39

P

Oddendale Hamlet

Oddendale Stone Circle

Approx 1km

For detail see Landranger sheet 91

HOW TO GET THERE

If you are walking, continue on the track south from the western edge of Oddendale village.

If driving, park at the start of the track. The circle is a few hundred metres to the southwest. Proceed along the track, past the large area of limestone pavement, but not as far as the prominent stone cairn (Seal Howe), which you will see on the low summit to your left. After about 500 metres, the circle is about 200 metres off the track to the right.

Of all the circles visited, this proved the most difficult for the author to find, mainly because all the stones are fallen, and the fact that the recumbent stones lie in an area with patches of limestone pavement.

GAMELANDS

GAMELANDS Stone Circle
Grid reference NY 640082
Number of stones 33, although
originally there were probably about
40, set on a low bank. The stones are
made of the relatively indestructible
Shap Granite, as are most of the circles
in eastern Lakeland.
Diameter between 44.5 and 37.5
metres.
Age about 1800 to 1400 BC
Nearest village Orton; nearest town
Kendal.

Gamelands must have been an impressive monument when it was built

Though one of the largest circles described in this guide, Gamelands is perhaps the least visited. This is partly because it is outside the National Park, but as all the stones have fallen, it lacks the drama of Castlerigg, Swinside or Long Meg.

However, the stones in the circle are enormous, and when erect must have been an impressive sight.

Visitors are able to enjoy the peaceful setting and to quietly contemplate what might have been the function of this place almost 4000 years ago. What caused these primitive early farmers to assemble these enormous stones, long before our modern technology, 2000 years before Julius Caesar set foot on British soil? At one time Gamelands stone circle must have been mightily impressive. Today, in its most glorious setting below the limestone pavements of Knott Hill, it can still provide an awe-inspiring experience.

The stones at Gamelands are huge

HOW TO GET THERE

Gamelands stone circle is located about 1.5 km east of the village of Orton, northeast of Kendal, just outside the National Park.

From Orton leave the village going east on the B6261; after a few hundred metres take the minor road left to Raisebeck. Continue for 1.5 km (1 mile), then turn left on to a bridleway. Gamelands is 200 metres up the bridleway (Knott Lane) 200 metres, to the right. The limestone scar of Knott Hill is situated beyond. There is no access from the lane immediately adjacent to the circle, but the owners, Allan and Mark Mawson are happy for visitors to reach the circle via the second of the two gates, and then to proceed through an ungated gap in the next wall.

"Simple Map" showing location of

GAMELANDS STONE CIRCLE

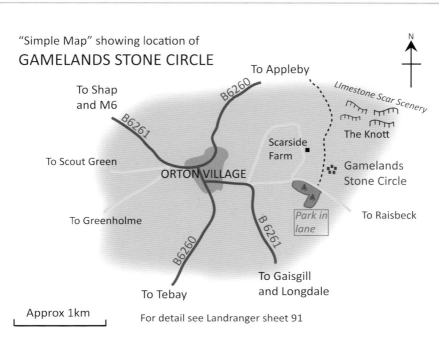

To Appleby

To Shap and M6

To Scout Green

Limestone Scar Scenery

The Knott

Scarside Farm

ORTON VILLAGE

Gamelands Stone Circle

To Greenholme

Park in lane

To Raisebeck

To Tebay

To Gaisgill and Longdale

Approx 1km

For detail see Landranger sheet 91

MAYBURGH HENGE

MAYBURY HENGE
Grid reference NY 519 284
KING ARTHUR'S ROUND TABLE
Grid reference NY 523 283
Mayburgh Henge and King Arthur's round table are not stone circles. However, they are of the same age, and are sufficiently impressive to be of considerable interest to the visitor, and so we include them.

Only an aerial view can show the sheer scale of Mayburgh Henge

Mayburgh Henge is a massive circular bank, up to 117 metres in diameter and varying from 2.5 to 5 metres tall. It is built entirely of millions of rounded river pebbles. As one climbs the embankment and peers inside, the impression is one of the enormity of the structure. It is like entering a stadium, and must have created an awe-inspiring spectacle for early man. There is a single entrance in the southeast of the bank and a single standing stone, 2.8 metres tall, in the centre, the sole remnant of 4 original stones. There were also four stones at the entrance.

The pebbles of which the henge is built are frequently exposed around the inside slopes, evidence of the immense task in the building of this structure. The henge is believed to be between 3000 and 4000 years old, the same age as the later stone circles.

48

KING ARTHUR'S ROUND TABLE

This structure pre-dates King Arthur by several thousand years, and is made up of an earthen bank, surrounded by a ditch. It is likely that it originally also included a spectacular, but now long-gone stone circle. Mayburgh Henge is thought to be slightly the older.

King Arthur's Round Table sliced through by the road to Pooley Bridge

The functions of the henge and the round table

There are no clear astronomical alignments in either monument, so it is assumed they were used for a combination of ritual functions and probably also as a market place. Mayburgh Henge was certainly an important place, as its construction required an enormous communal effort.

Both structures give the impression that they were created as places where events were staged. Mayburgh Henge does have the feel of a stadium, and its slopes could have held many thousands of people.

The Round Table also has the appearance of a platform on which events, ritualistic, sporting or merely commercial were held.

Spend time in both these sites and dwell on what you think their functions might have been.

"Simple Map" showing location of
MAYBURGH HENGE and
KING ARTHUR'S ROUND TABLE

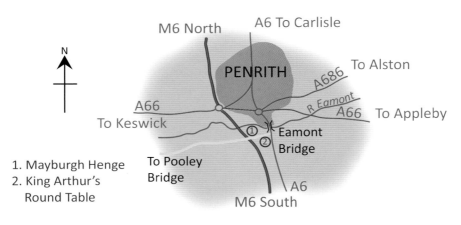

M6 North   A6 To Carlisle

N

PENRITH   To Alston

A686

A66   R Eamont   A66   To Appleby
To Keswick

① Eamont
② Bridge

1. Mayburgh Henge   To Pooley
2. King Arthur's   Bridge
   Round Table   A6

M6 South

Approx 1km   For detail see Landranger sheet 90

The Penrith Millennium Rock

Detail of the Millenium Rock showing "phenocrysts"

HOW TO GET THERE

Travel south out of Penrith on the A6 to Eamont Bridge. Turn first right after the bridge, on to the B 5320 road for Pooley Bridge. Mayburgh Henge is about 400m to the west, close to the M6 motorway, whilst King Arthur's Round Table is right next to the junction. The monuments are open all of the time, under the control of English Heritage and admission is free. On the way there you pass Penrith's newest megalith, a 50 tonne lump of Shap granite, commemorating the millennium. It allows you a chance to inspect the characteristics of this special rock.

50

OTHER CUMBRIAN CIRCLES NOT FEATURED

The stone circles featured in this book include the most visitable and the best known. However, throughout the area there are many other sites, some of which we list below.

SOUTH AND WEST CUMBRIA

Bleaberry Haws	Grid Ref SD 264 946	Near Torver.
Lacra	Grid Ref. SD 150 813	West of Millom.
Gretigate	Grid Ref. NY 058 037	West of Gosforth
Hird Wood	Grid Ref. NY 417 059	Northeast of Ambleside close to A592.
Studfold	Grid Ref. NY 040 223	Southeast of Workington
The Beacon	Grid Ref. SD 280 842	South of Lowick Green
The Kirk	Grid Ref. SD 251 827	West of the Duddon Estuary.
Casterton	Grid Ref. SD 639 800	Northeast of Kirkby Lonsdale

NORTH CUMBRIA

Glassonby	Grid Ref. NY 573 393	Northwest of the hamlet of Glassonby
Broomrigg	Grid Ref. NY548 467	East of Ainstable, south of Carlisle.
Leacet Hill	Grid Ref. NY563 263	Southeast of Penrith
Swarth Fell	Grid Ref. NY 457 192	East side of Ullswater

WHERE TO GET MORE INFORMATION

This little book is not intended to be comprehensive, but more of a "taster", to get you started. Once you have visited a few sites, you may wish either to access more points of view on the Lake District circles, or perhaps to go further afield.
There are other books on the subject, though many are out of print, and may have to be obtained from your library or perhaps from a second-hand bookshop.
Probably most valuable is the web, and there are numerous sites.
The bibliography is intended to move you further along the road in this fascinating subject.

BOOKS

Clare, Tom: Prehistoric Monuments of the Lake District
Burl A.: The Stone Circles of Britain, Ireland and Brittany
Burl A. & Thom A.: Megalithic Rings; Plans and Data for 229 Monuments in Britain
Thom, A.: Megalithic Remains in Britain, Brittany and Ireland
Waterhouse, John: The Stone Circles of Cumbria.

WEB-SITES

www.megalith.ukf.net
(The Megalithic map, showing all UK sites)

www.stonepages.com

www.britainexpress.com

www.stone-circles.org.uk

www.english-heritage.org.uk

www.mysteriousbritain.co.uk

www.megalithic.co.uk

www.themodernantiquarian.com